TABLE OF CONTENTS

WILDFIRE!

Weeks of hot weather cause plants to **wilt** and crumble. Finally, storm clouds rumble. Lightning sparks a fire in a dry tree. Wind fans the flames, making them spread. Run! It's a wildfire!

WORLD'S WORST NATURAL DISASTERS

THE WORLD'S WORST
WILDFIRES

by Tracy Nelson Maurer

CAPSTONE PRESS
a capstone imprint

Blazers Books are published by Capstone Press,
1710 Roe Crest Drive, North Mankato, Minnesota 56003
www.mycapstone.com

Library of Congress Cataloging-in-Publication Data is available on the
Library of Congress website.
ISBN: 978-1-5435-5479-3 (library hardcover) — 978-1-5435-5903-3
(paperback) — 978-1-5435-5483-0 (eBook PDF)

Summary: Learn about the world's most devastating wildfires.

Editorial Credits
Gena Chester, editor; Julie Peters, designer;
Jo Miller, media researcher; Tori Abraham, production specialist

Photo Credits
AP Images, 14–15; Bridgeman Images: Look and Learn/Private
Collection/Illustrated Papers Collection, 8–9; Getty Images: Don
Johnston, 22–23; Mary Evans Picture Library, 10–11; Minnesota
Historical Society Photographic Collection, 20–21; Newscom: MCT/
Darin Oswald, 26–27, Reuters/Ronen Zvulun, 12–13, UPI/POOL,
24–25; Shutterstock: BrittanyNY, 16–17, Christian Roberts-Olsen,
Cover, leonello calvetti, Cover, 3, 31, Sergei Drozd, 18–19, Sundays
Photography, 28–29, Tomas Nevesely, 6–7, yelantsevv, 4–5

Design Elements
Shutterstock: Puckung, xpixel, yelantsevv

wilt—to droop; some plants lose water and bend over in heat

fuel—anything that can be burned to give off energy

BURNING OUT OF CONTROL

Every year, **wilderness** areas burn out of control around the world. Lightning can cause wildfires. People may also start the blazes. Campfires that aren't put out cause many wildfires. Sparks from machines, such as trains and all-terrain vehicles (ATVs), can also start wildfires.

FACT Wildfire strength depends on the weather, wind, and how much fuel is nearby.

A NIGHT OF DEADLY FIRE

The Peshtigo Fire

Location:
Wisconsin and
Michigan, USA

Date:
October 8, 1871

Burned:
1.2 million acres
(48,562 hectares)

= 1 million
acres

One fall evening, a huge blaze started in eastern Wisconsin. A **brushfire** started while workers cleared land for railroad tracks. Flames soon roared through towns. More than 1,200 people died.

FACT

The Peshtigo Fire jumped across Green Bay, a body of water between Wisconsin and Michigan.

FIRE ZONE

The Black Friday
Bushfires

Location:
Victoria, Australia

Date:
January 13, 1939

Burned:
Nearly 5 million acres
(2 million hectares)

= 1 million
acres

Fires **ignite** easily during dry weather in Australia's **bush**. Careless use of fire set off a series of blazes. The flames scorched more than half of the state of Victoria. The disaster killed 71 people.

FACT

Wind carried ash from the bushfires as far as New Zealand, about 1,300 miles (2,100 kilometers).

ignite—to set fire to something

bush—the large, wild areas of Australia where few people live

INTERNATIONAL FIRE FIGHTING

Mount Carmel
Wildfire

Location:
Haifa, Israel

Date:
December 2–5, 2010

Burned:
More than 7,400 acres
(2,995 hectares)

= 1 thousand
acres

Dry weather and winds blew small blazes into fierce wildfires on Mount Carmel. More than 13 **nations** sent aircrafts and firefighters to stop the fires. At least 40 people died.

FACT

Israel saw major wildfires again in 2016, most likely due to **arson**.

nation—a group of people with the same language, customs, and government

arson—the crime of setting fire to a building or property on purpose

BLAZING MORE THAN A MONTH

The Black
Saturday Fire

Location:
Victoria, Australia

Date:
February 7, 2009

Burned:
1.1 million acres
(450,000 hectares)

= 1 million acres

During a heatwave, several small fires began in Australia's bush. Two days later, the fires combined into a wall of flames. The blaze topped 328 feet (100 meters). The fire burned for more than a month. The disaster killed 173 people.

About 84 percent of wildfires are caused by humans.

CALIFORNIA'S FIRESTORM

The Thomas Fire

Location:
Ventura,
California, USA

Date:
December 4, 2017–
January 12, 2018

Burned:
281,893 acres
(114,078 hectares)

= 50 thousand
acres

High winds fanned fires near the mountain city of Ventura. Flames soon rushed into neighborhoods. Two people died and more than 1,000 homes and buildings burned.

The Thomas Fire grew so hot and big that it caused its own weather, making it a true **firestorm**.

firestorm—a large fire in which strong winds cause bigger flames

THE WORLD'S LARGEST WILDFIRES

Siberian Taiga Fires

Location:
Siberia, Russia

Date:
July 29–
September 2, 2003

Burned:
47 million acres
(19 million hectares)

🔥🔥🔥🔥🔥 🔥🔥🔥🔥🔥
🔥🔥🔥🔥🔥 🔥🔥🔥🔥🔥
🔥🔥🔥🔥🔥 🔥🔥🔥🔥🔥
🔥🔥🔥🔥🔥 🔥🔥🔥🔥🔥
🔥🔥🔥🔥🔥
🔥🔥

🔥 = 1 million
acres

Hot weather caused waves of wildfires in **remote** parts of Russia. Dry forests burned for months. Hazy smoke covered all of Europe and Asia for weeks afterward.

remote—far away, isolated, or distant

TOWERS OF FLAMES

The Great
Hinckley Fire

Location:
Hinckley, Minnesota,
USA

Date:
September 1, 1894

Burned:
350,000 acres
(141,600 hectares)

🔥 🔥 🔥 🔥

🔥 🔥 🔥

🔥 = 50 thousand
acres

Hinckley's lumber company stood near the railroad tracks. Rising temperatures and strong winds combined with sawdust and lumber to spark wildfires. Swirling towers of flames reached 200 feet (61 m) high. A total of 418 people died.

FACT

The Great Hinckley Fire was so hot that it melted railcar wheels to the tracks.

CANADA'S SMOKE SIGNALS

The Northwest Territories Fires

Location:
Northern Canada

Date:
Summer 2014

Burned:
8.6 million acres
(3.5 million hectares)

= 1 million acres

Experts believe humans caused 385 fires one summer in Northern Canada. More than 100 fires raged there at the same time. Amazingly, no one died in these record fires.

FACT

Smoky air from wildfires can make breathing difficult. The smoke may damage airways and lungs.

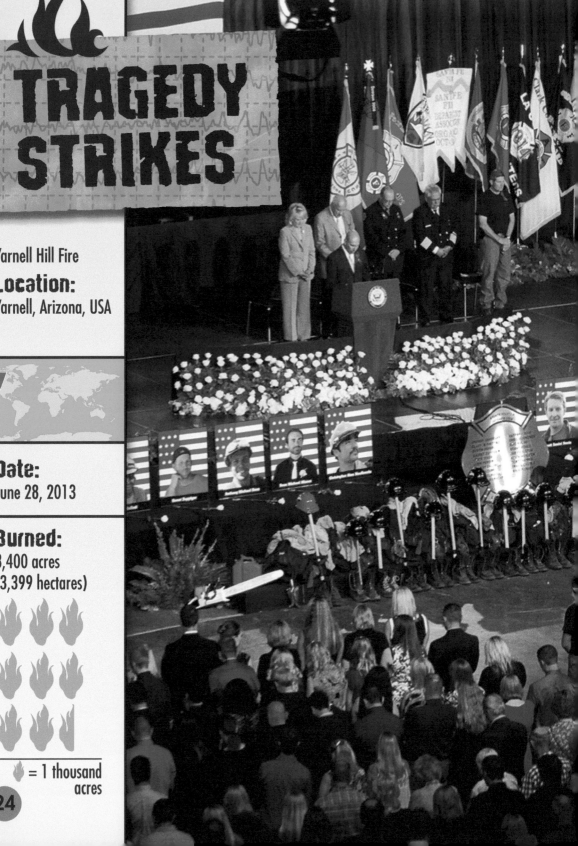

TRAGEDY STRIKES

Yarnell Hill Fire

Location:
Yarnell, Arizona, USA

Date:
June 28, 2013

Burned:
8,400 acres
(3,399 hectares)

= 1 thousand acres

Twenty **elite** firefighters tried to fight a desert wildfire in central Arizona. One firefighter took a lookout spot. The others cleared fuel. Suddenly, the flames switched direction and trapped the team. Nineteen firemen died. Only one survived.

FACT

Experts believe the fire covered about 100 yards (91 m) in 19 seconds.

elite—the part or group having the highest quality or importance

FIGHTING WILDFIRES

Fighting fires is dangerous work. Firefighters attack wildfires by clearing fuel. They use aircraft to dump water on flames. There are specially trained fighters called smoke jumpers. They leap from airplanes to reach fires in remote areas.

FACT

Firefighters are trained to work safely as they protect lives and homes.

PREVENTING WILDFIRES

Everyone can help **prevent** wildfires. Use these tips to help make a difference.

1. Do not play with matches.

2. Never leave a campfire burning. Dump water on it to be sure it is out.

3. Remove fuel, such as dry trees and shrubs, surrounding buildings.

prevent—to keep from happening

GLOSSARY

arson (AR-suhn)—the crime of setting fire to a building or property on purpose

brushfire (BRUHSH-fyr)—a fire involving low-growing plants

bush (BUSH)—the large, wild areas of Australia where few people live

elite (i-LEET)—the part or group having the highest quality or importance

firestorm (FYR STORM)—a large fire that burns so hot it creates its own weather

fuel (FYOOL)—anything that can be burned to give off energy

ignite (ig-NITE)—to set fire to something

nation (NAY-shuhn)—a group of people with the same language, customs, and government

prevent (pri-VENT)—to keep from happening

remote (ri-MOHT)—far away, isolated, or distant

wilderness (WIL-dur-niss)—a natural, undeveloped region

wilt (WIHLT)—to droop; some plants lose water and bend over in heat

READ MORE

Furgang, Kathy. *Wildfires*. National Geographic Readers. National Geographic Children's Books, 2015.

Kodas, Michael. *Megafire: The Race to Extinguish a Deadly Epidemic of Flame.* New York: Houghton Mifflin, 2017.

Simon, Seymour. *Wildfires*. New York: Harper, an imprint of HarperCollins Publishers, 2016.

INTERNET SITES

Use Facthound to find Internet sites related to this book.

Visit www.facthound.com.

Just type in 9781543554793 and go!

Check out projects, games and lots more at
www.capstonekids.com

CRITICAL THINKING QUESTIONS

1. What causes wildfires?

2. Why might firefighting be dangerous work?

3. Why do you think fuel, air temperature, and wind speed and direction might affect a wildfire?

INDEX